Claudia Joyal Laplante

21 DAYS TO LEARN TO knit

× *daily practice* ×

× *step-by-step instructions* ×

× *8 projects* ×

21 Days to Learn to Knit

First published in the United States in 2026 by Stash Books, an imprint of C&T Publishing, Inc., P.O. Box 1456, Lafayette, CA 94549

21 jours pour apprendre à tricoter © 2024 by Éditions Marie Claire - Société d'Information et de Créations (SIC)

This edition of "*21 jours pour apprendre à tricoter*" first published in France by Éditions Marie Claire in 2024 is published by arrangement with Marie Claire.

PUBLISHER: Amy Barrett-Daffin

CREATIVE DIRECTOR: Gailen Runge

SENIOR EDITOR: Roxane Cerda

EDITOR: Madison Moore

ENGLISH LANGUAGE COVER DESIGNER AND LAYOUT ARTIST: April Mostek

ENGLISH TRANSLATION: Kristy Darling Finder

PRODUCTION COORDINATORS: Casey Dukes and Zinnia Heinzmann

EDITORIAL DIRECTOR: Adeline Lobut

EDITORIAL COORDINATOR: Isabelle Misery

EDITING: Julie Bez

CREATION, PRODUCTION, EXPLANATIONS: Claudia Joyal Laplante

PHOTOGRAPHY: Fabrice Besse

STYLING: Sonia Roy

TECHNICAL REVISION: Claude from @hellolucette

COVER AND GRAPHIC DESIGN: Claire Morel Fatio

LAYOUT: Littopia

All rights reserved. No part of this work covered by the copyright hereon may be used in any form or reproduced by any means—graphic, electronic, or mechanical, including photocopying, recording, taping, or information storage and retrieval systems—without written permission from the publisher. These designs may be used to make items for personal use only and may not be used for the purpose of personal profit. Items created to benefit nonprofit groups, or that will be publicly displayed, must be conspicuously labeled with the following credit: "Designs copyright © 2024 by Éditions Marie Claire - Société d'Information et de Créations (SIC) from the book *21 Days to Learn to Knit* from C&T Publishing, Inc." Permission for all other purposes must be requested in writing from C&T Publishing, Inc.

Attention Teachers: C&T Publishing, Inc., encourages the use of our books as texts for teaching. You can find lesson plans for many of our titles at ctpub.com or contact us at ctinfo@ctpub.com.

We take great care to ensure that the information included in our products is accurate and presented in good faith, but no warranty is provided, nor are results guaranteed. Having no control over the choices of materials or procedures used, neither the author nor C&T Publishing, Inc., shall have any liability to any person or entity with respect to any loss or damage caused directly or indirectly by the information contained in this book. For your convenience, we post an up-to-date listing of corrections on our website (ctpub.com). If a correction is not already noted, please contact our customer service department at ctinfo@ctpub.com or P.O. Box 1456, Lafayette, CA 94549.

Trademark (™) and registered trademark (®) names are used throughout this book. Rather than use the symbols with every occurrence of a trademark or registered trademark name, we are using the names only in the editorial fashion and to the benefit of the owner, with no intention of infringement.

ISBN: 978-1-64403-629-7

Printed in China

10 9 8 7 6 5 4 3 2 1

LEARN TO KNIT

INTRODUCTION

Learn to knit in 21 days: that's the challenge I present to you with this book. You will be guided through 21 days of learning and practicing that you will then apply to projects with step-by-step instructions.

Knitting is an art that demands practice and patience. You may need more than a single day to master a particular technique, and certain projects require more time for completion. Knit a little every day, following the steps in this book at your own pace you will then gain the knowledge and confidence you need to take on any project you wish.

Happy knitting!

Claudia

ECRU
041191 1359 01
135
3 307673 933725
PHIL MERINOS 3,5

GLOSSARY

Binding off
Also called *casting off*, this creates the last row of your knitting, the final edge of the work.

Casting on
This creates the first row of knitting, the foundation of stitches on the needle. It is not counted as an actual knit row.

Edge stitch
These are the stitches on the right and left sides of your knitting, the first and last stitches in a row which give a beautiful finish to the piece. For example, you can use the knit stitch on the edges of each row for a garter stitch edge. Or you can slip the first stitch as you would for purling and knit the last stitch to create a chain stitch edge.

Row
This is formed by all the stitches on the needle.

Slip, knit, pass over (skpo)
This is a decrease. Slip one stitch, knit the next one normally, and pass the slipped stitch over the knit stitch.

Slip 1, knit 2 together, pass over
This is the same thing as the slip, knit, pass over (skpo), but you knit two stitches together instead of only one, decreasing the row by two stitches overall. This may be abbreviated as sl1-k2tog-psso, sk2tpo, or simply sk2p.

Slipped stitch
Move the stitch from the left needle to the right needle without knitting.

Stitch
Each loop of yarn on the needle represents one stitch.

Work stitches as they appear
Also written *knit the knits* and *purl the purls*, this means to knit in knit stitches and purl in purl stitches. The opposite is to *knit the purls* and *purl the knits*.

Yarn over
This allows you to create openwork in your knitting, or to add a stitch as it is knit. Wrap the yarn around the needle before knitting the stitch.

ABBREVIATIONS

RS
the right side of the work

WS
the wrong side of the work

k
knit stitch

p
purl stitch

r
row

k2tog
knit 2 stitches together (see Day 5)

ssk
(slip, slip, knit): Slip a stitch as if to knit, slip the next stitch as if to knit, insert the left needle, from left to right, into the strands before the 2 slipped stitches and knit together (see Day 5).

inc
increase (see Day 9)

...
everything between the 2 asterisks is repeated the number of times indicated

m
marker; Markers are placed on the needle to mark a section or a particular stitch and slipped to the right needle each time it comes up (see Day 6).

pm
place the marker on the needle (see Day 6)

sm
slip the marker

THE MATERIALS

To get started with knitting, you need needles and yarn. That seems simple enough—but which should you choose?

THE YARN

Your choice of yarn will inform your choice of needles. Most yarns are sold with a label that tells you the recommended needle size. This indicated size is a good place to start, but bear in mind that you can knit the same yarn with different sizes of needles depending on the effect you want to achieve with your knitting (dense, flowing, lacy...). The yarns used in this book mostly fall into the category of *bulky* or *worsted*, a thicker yarn that will allow you to clearly see your stitches and make rapid progress in your work. The last project calls for *fine* or *sport* yarn to create more lightweight, delicate stitches with a more detailed appearance.

Note: A table of the various yarn categories and their different names can be found at the end of the book.

The yarn fiber can also significantly affect your projects: wool, acrylic, cotton, alpaca, etc. Each fiber presents pros and cons, and depending on the project you want to make, certain yarns will be more appropriate than others. For this book, I've decided to work with merino wool yarn, known for its softness and lightness. If you want to knit with a different kind of yarn, I recommend going for either acrylic or an acrylic/wool blend to achieve a similar texture.

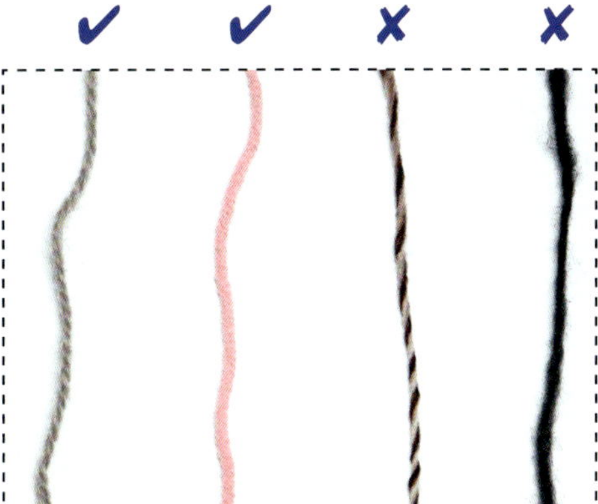

Tip: When learning to knit, it's best to use two-ply (or twisted) yarn instead of single-ply yarn, which has a tendency to pill and makes undoing stitches difficult. You should also choose a lighter color when starting out as it is harder to see the stitches (and especially the mistakes!) with dark yarn.

THE NEEDLES

There are several factors to consider when choosing your needles.

THE MATERIAL

Wooden or plastic needles are often the best choice for beginning knitters since they create more friction than metal ones, which helps prevent stitches from accidentally slipping and dropping from the needles.

THE SIZE

Needle size is based on your choice of yarn (see above). Be aware that sizes are indicated in millimeters in Europe and by a different system in the US. You will need US size 10 needles (6mm) for all the projects in this book, with the exception of the last project which requires US size 6 needles (4mm).

THE TYPE

Traditionally, knitting is taught using long straight needles. Although these continue to be used, these days circular needles are widely adopted for their versatility: with them, you can knit flat or in the round for all the lessons! You will need 16″ (40cm) circular needles to make the neck warmer and beanie.

For everything else, you can use straight or circular needles depending on your personal preference.

Note: When buying circular needles, you will see that you have the option of either fixed or interchangeable needles. The benefit of interchangeable needles is that you can buy the length of cable and the right size needles for a project. Then for the next project, you can simply buy a different length cable or different sized needles to mix-and-match. This way, you will build a set over time.

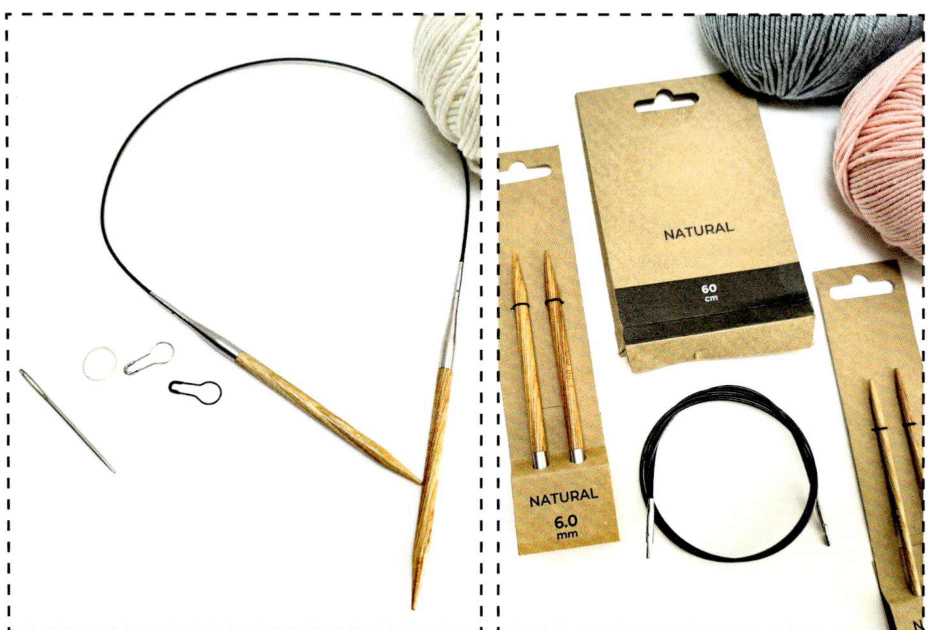

OTHER ESSENTIAL TOOLS

- A pair of scissors.

- A tapestry or yarn needle: this looks like a regular sewing needle but thicker, with a larger eye and a blunt tip.

- Stitch markers: any little round thing that can be slipped onto your needle (bulb safety pins, little knotted loops of thread, or knit-specific markers etc.).

Lesson

THE KNIT STITCH

To get started, you need to learn how to cast on: the classic method is the *long tail cast-on.*

THE LONG TAIL CAST-ON

1

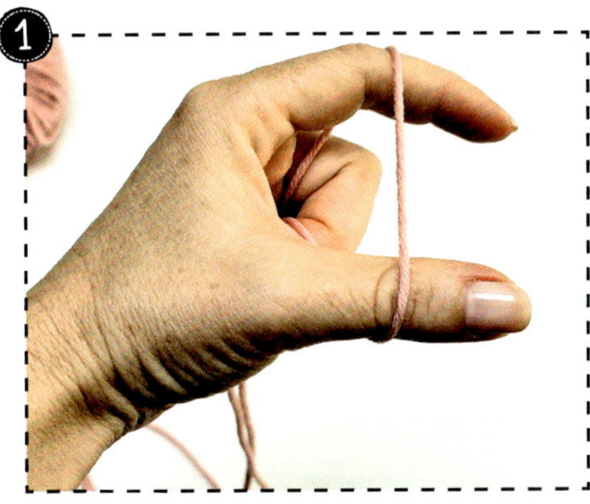

Unroll a length of yarn 3 times the width of your final project. Form a C with your left index finger and thumb. Run the yarn over your thumb and index finger, and close your other three fingers over the 2 ends of the yarn to form a triangle. (The loose end of the yarn is over your thumb, while the yarn attached to the skein is over your index finger.)

2

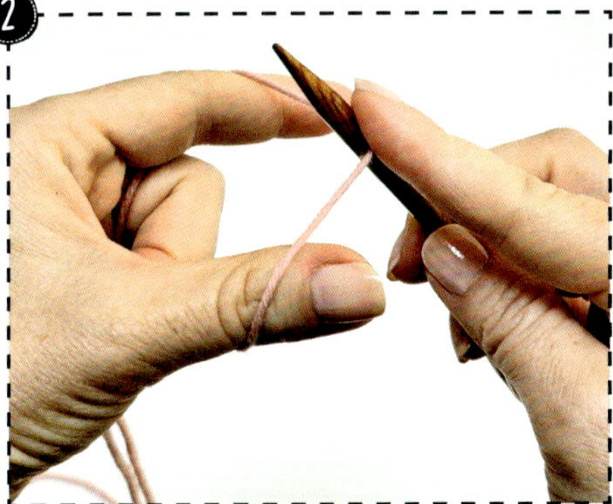

Take the needle in your right hand, place it under the yarn, and press your right index finger on the yarn to hold it in place.

Slide the needle into the loop around your thumb from the bottom up.

Pass your needle over the yarn on your index finger.

Pull the yarn from your index finger through the loop on your thumb.

Release the loop on your thumb.

Tighten the yarn on the needle by placing your thumb back under the yarn to create a stitch. Repeat Steps 3–7 until you have the desired number of stitches.

Note: The long tail cast-on creates a row of knit stitches. When you turn your work over to begin knitting, this will be row 2. The end of the cast-on yarn will be on the left when you knit on the right side of the work.

THE KNIT STITCH

1

Take the needle with the stitches in your left hand. With the empty needle in your right hand, place the yarn behind it and insert the needle into the front loop of the first stitch, from front to back, making an X with the needles.

2

Wrap the yarn around the right needle counterclockwise, from back to front.

3

Using the right needle, draw the yarn forward through the stitch.

4

Gently drop the first stitch from the left needle, keeping the remaining stitches on the needle. Repeat Steps 1–4 for each stitch until the end of the row. When all the stitches have been knit, turn your work over and start a new row, beginning again at Step 1.

Note: When you make rows of only knit stitches on both sides of the work, this is called a garter stitch. To get your bearings when counting rows of garter stitch, you need to count the waves; these are created when you knit 2 rows: 1 wave = 2 rows.

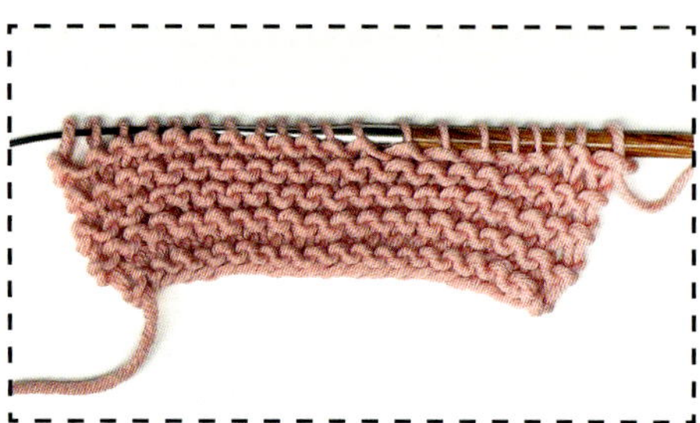

TODAY'S PRACTICE

Knit rows of knit stitch until you feel more comfortable with this stitch and the yarn tension—which should be tight enough that the fabric is not see-through, but loose enough that it is easy to insert the needle into each stitch. Count your stitches at the end of each row to make sure you're knitting every stitch and not adding any extra. Don't stop if you notice mistakes; continue and watch your work improve over time.

Tip: Pay close attention when beginning a new row. It often happens that the yarn goes over the needle, giving the impression of 2 stitches. Run the yarn under your left needle and backward to reveal the first stitch.

✔

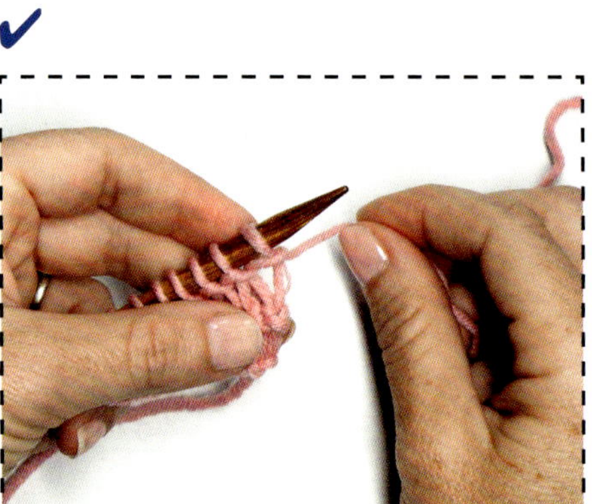

✗

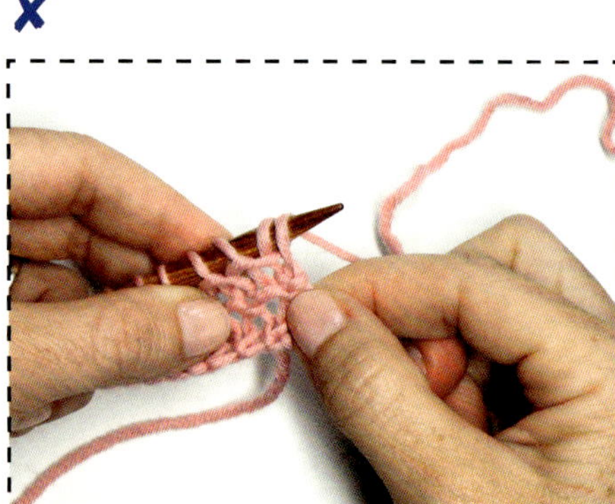

THE BASIC BIND-OFF

To finish your work, you need to know how to stop your stitches. You can then weave in the yarn tail (see page 79).

1

Knit in the first two stitches on the left needle at the beginning of a new row.

2

Insert the left needle into the first stitch on the right needle and lift the stitch. Hold the second stitch in place with your index finger.

3

Carry the first stitch over the second stitch and over the tip of the right needle to drop it off the needle. There is still one stitch on the right needle. Knit the following stitch. Now, you again have two stitches on the right needle.

4

Repeat Steps 2–4 until you only have one stitch on the right needle and none on the left. Cut the yarn, leaving about a 4″ (10cm) tail, and pull the loop to bring the yarn tail through the stitch.

day 3

Project FRINGED COASTER

MATERIELS

- Size 10 needles (6mm)
- 1 ball of bulky or worsted merino yarn (Blush)
- Yarn needle and scissors

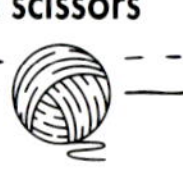

SKILLS

- Casting on
- Knit stitch
- Binding off

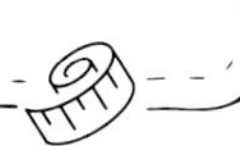

STEP-BY-STEP

THE COASTER

- Cast on 20 sts.

- k every st for 31 rows (16 waves in total)

- Bind off.

THE FRINGES

- Cut 40 pieces of yarn each about 6″ (15cm) long.

- Fold the yarn pieces in half. Using a crochet hook or yarn needle, insert a piece of yarn through the bottom of each cast-on stitch, then run the 2 ends through the loop to secure the fringe. (Include the beginning and end of the working yarn in the nearest fringe.)

- Repeat the previous step along the bind-off row.

- Even up the fringes using the scissors.

1 dl

Lesson

THE PURL STITCH

THE PURL STITCH

The purl stitch is the second and final stitch you need to know in order to create a wide variety of designs.

1

After casting on and knitting one row, take the needle with the stitches in your left hand. With the empty needle in your right hand, place the yarn in front of it and insert the needle into the front loop of the first stitch, from right to left, creating an X with the right needle in front.

2

Wrap the yarn around the right needle counterclockwise, from back to front.

Using the right needle, draw the yarn backward through the stitch.

Gently drop the first stitch from the left needle, keeping the remaining stitches on the needle. Repeat Steps 1–4 until the end of the row. When you have worked all the stitches, turn the work over and start a new row, beginning again at Step 1.

Note: When you make rows of only purl stitches in both directions, you will see that once again you've created the garter stitch, because the purl stitch is, in fact, the reverse of a knit stitch!

THE STOCKINETTE STITCH

Stockinette stitch, also called the stocking or jersey stitch, is the most used stitch in knitting. It is made by alternating rows of knit stitches and purl stitches.

It's easy to recognize the right and wrong sides of your work in stockinette since the right side will have a pattern of little Vs (photo 1) while the wrong side will have a series of waves (photo 2).

To count rows of stockinette stitch, you simply need to count all the Vs in one column (also known as a "wale"), including the stitch on the needle.

TODAY'S PRACTICE

Cast on 20 stitches.

Alternate rows of knit stitches and purl stitches until you have a good understanding of the 2 stitches and know how to recognize them. Take the time to observe how a knit or purl stitch looks on the row just below the needle. Knowing how to read your knitting will be your greatest tool as you learn. Leave this swatch on your needles for tomorrow's practice.

Note: Stockinette stitch has a tendency to roll in on itself; this is natural and unavoidable. This is why it is often paired with a border to stabilize it. However, you can also use this natural rolling of the stockinette stitch to create, for example, a rim on a beanie or a very simple scarf with colored yarn.

Lesson DECREASING

To create shapes while knitting, we use decreases and increases. Today, you will learn the two basic types of decreases for knit rows.

RIGHT-LEANING DECREASE: KNIT 2 STITCHES TOGETHER (K2TOG)

1

To create the k2tog decrease, insert your right needle into the front loop of the 2nd stitch and then the 1st stitch on the left needle. Then, knit the 2 stitches together the same way you would knit 1.

You will now see under your stitch that 2 columns of Vs come together to form a single column. The left V will be above the right V, which is what makes this decrease lean to the right.

LEFT-LEANING DECREASE: SLIP-SLIP-KNIT (SSK)

2

To create the ssk decrease, insert your right needle into a stitch as if to knit, but slip the stitch over to the right needle without knitting, slip a second stitch the same way. Then, insert the left needle into the 2 front loops of the 2 slipped stitches, and knit them together.

You will now see under your stitch that 2 columns of Vs come together to form a single column. The right V will be above the left V, which is what makes this decrease lean to the left.

Note: You will often see skpo (slip, knit, pass over) on patterns, which is a left-leaning decrease that is interchangeable with the ssk. You can choose whichever you prefer (see the glossary for skpo instructions).

TODAY'S PRACTICE

On the stockinette swatch you began yesterday, create symmetrical decreases on each side as follows:

R 1—k2, ssk, k until 4 st from the end, k2tog, k2
R 2—p

Repeat rows 1 and 2 four more times. You now have 10 stitches remaining on your needles. Take the time to really look over your work to recognize the decreases and their effect on your knitting.

Lesson LIFELINE AND STITCH MARKERS

Learning to knit inevitably involves making mistakes. But don't worry, you can almost always fix your mistakes without having to undo all of your precious work.

THE LIFELINE

Allow me to introduce you to your new best friend: the lifeline. As indicated by its name, this will always be there to save you if you find yourself in trouble.

1

All you need to do is insert a fine, sturdy yarn through every stitch on your knitting needle using a yarn needle.

Choose your lifeline in a contrasting color so that it will not get confused with the stitches of your work-in-progress. This yarn will remain in place as long as you continue to knit. Since it runs through the stitches of a row, if you need to undo your knitting, the lifeline will preserve the stitches of this row so you can reinsert your knitting needle and resume knitting at this step in the pattern.

You can insert a lifeline after every successfully completed step in a project before tackling the next stage, or simply every 10 rows, for example. When you put in a new lifeline, you can remove the previous one by gently pulling. This trick will give you the courage to try out more complex techniques and stitches, knowing that your work will not be lost if you don't succeed!

TODAY'S PRACTICE

Insert a lifeline into your work. Knit a few rows, then take a deep breath and remove the needle from your work. Undo your knitting until you reach the lifeline and reinsert your knitting needle through the stitches where the lifeline runs through them. After practicing this technique on a swatch, you will have no fear using it on a more important project.

Note: Running yarn through your stitches is also the technique you will use for placing stitches on hold. In that situation, the stitches will be slipped onto the yarn and not remain on the needle. If you only have one pair of knitting needles and want to continue practicing with this piece on your next lesson day, put your work on hold using a lifeline so you can use your needles on tomorrow's project!

day 6

STITCH MARKERS

When knitting a piece with different sections on a single row (ex.: a garter stitch border on a piece done in stockinette), put a stitch marker on your needle to demarcate these sections. You will need to slip this marker whenever you reach it, on every row, which will remind you to change stitches. Markers are also useful to mark where you need to decrease or increase. Never hesitate to use however many markers you need to make reading your knitting easier. There's no such thing as too many!

The abbreviation "m" will be used for markers in project instructions. Please see the Glossary and Abbreviations section for a complete list.

Note: If you run a lifeline through a row with markers, don't put the yarn through the markers, unless you want to keep your section borders clear if you have to undo your work!

3

Project MUG COZY

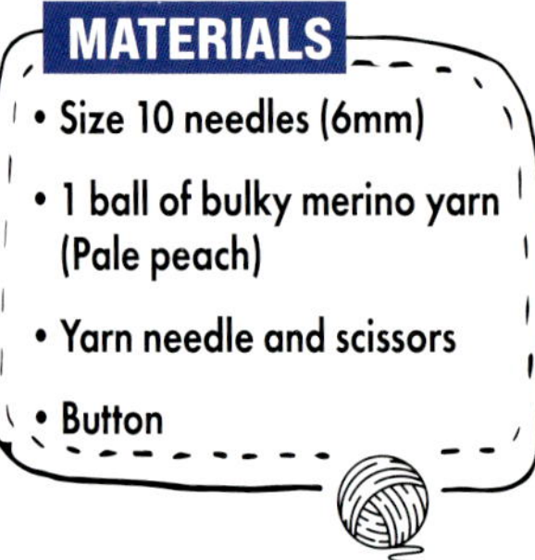

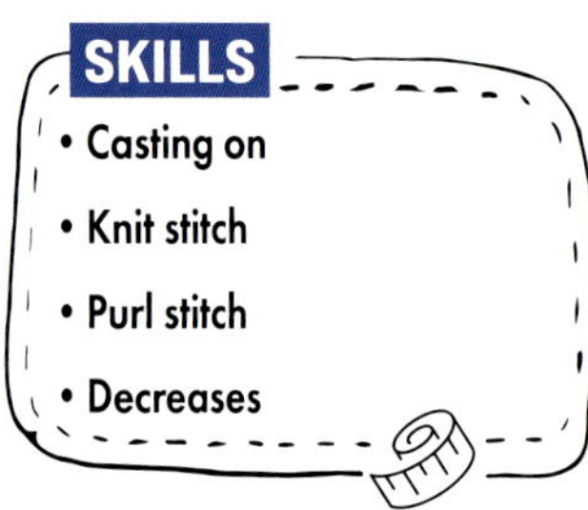

Note: Make sure to correctly position your working yarn before changing stitches for the purling rows by running the yarn between the 2 needles (yarn behind for knits, yarn in front for purls).

STEP-BY-STEP

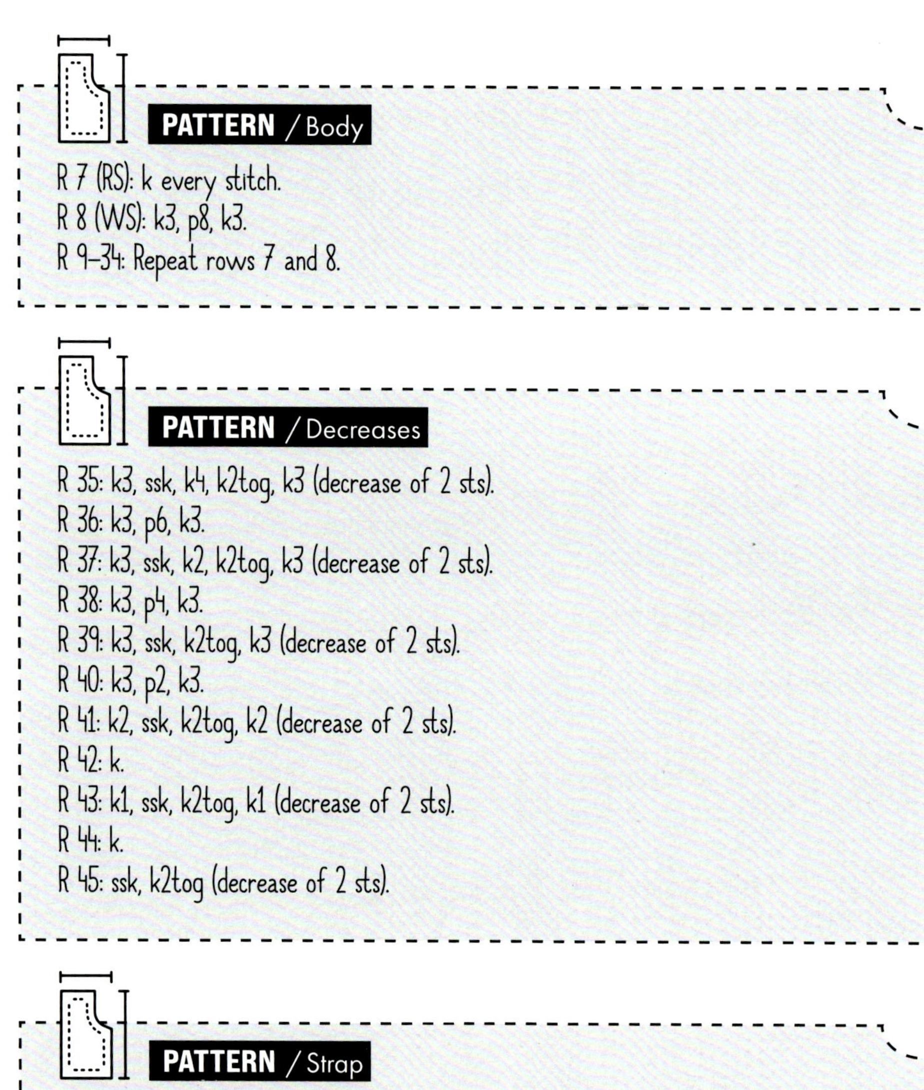

PATTERN / Body

R 7 (RS): k every stitch.
R 8 (WS): k3, p8, k3.
R 9–34: Repeat rows 7 and 8.

PATTERN / Decreases

R 35: k3, ssk, k4, k2tog, k3 (decrease of 2 sts).
R 36: k3, p6, k3.
R 37: k3, ssk, k2, k2tog, k3 (decrease of 2 sts).
R 38: k3, p4, k3.
R 39: k3, ssk, k2tog, k3 (decrease of 2 sts).
R 40: k3, p2, k3.
R 41: k2, ssk, k2tog, k2 (decrease of 2 sts).
R 42: k.
R 43: k1, ssk, k2tog, k1 (decrease of 2 sts).
R 44: k.
R 45: ssk, k2tog (decrease of 2 sts).

PATTERN / Strap

R 46–54: k.

FINISHING

Cut the yarn. Using the yarn needle, run the yarn through the 2 remaining stitches. Next, create a loop at the end of your work by sewing the yarn onto the wrong side at the base of your last decreases.

Weave in the ends of your yarn, then wash and block the project to prevent rolling (see Tips and Tricks, page 76). Lastly, with a piece of yarn and a sewing needle, sew the button in the center of the garter stitch edging at the start of your work.

Lesson
CHANGING SKEINS
OR COLORS

While working on a project, you may need to add a new skein or ball of yarn. The best place to do this is at the beginning of a row. Start by measuring how much yarn you have left; if you have less than 3 times the width of your project, you will not have enough yarn to finish the row. Take a new ball of yarn and simply start knitting. The first stitches will be loose, so you can pull slightly on the ends of the yarn to tighten them. After ten or so stitches, stop and make a loose knot with the 2 yarn ends to hold them together (1). When you've finished your knitting, you can untie the knot and hide the loose ends as explained in the Tips and Tricks section (page 76).

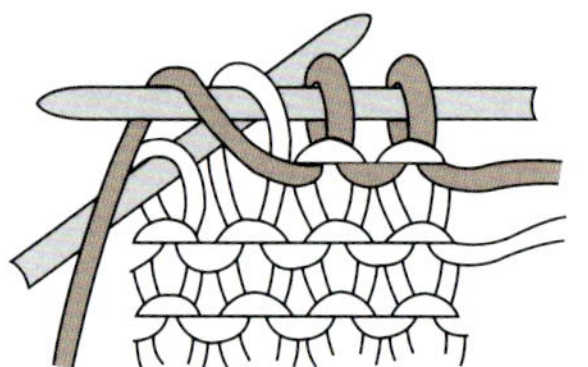

1

Use the exact same technique to change colors

Note: If you want to make thin stripes (2 rows, for example) with 2 colors, don't cut your yarn. Leave it on hold at the end of your row, knit 2 rows with the second color and return to your 1st yarn, making sure not to pull too tight so as to maintain the right tension of your knitting. This way, you'll have a lot fewer yarn tails to weave in.

2

TODAY'S PRACTICE

Have some fun changing colors with yarns you have at home. You can do this with both the garter and stockinette stitch to see the effect changing colors has on the right and wrong sides of these two stitches.

Lesson INCREASING

You already know about decreases, so today you will learn how to increase.

The simplest increase is called the yarn over. Though very simple, this technique creates a visible hole in your knitting; it is therefore very useful when you want to make lacy patterns. We will come back to this subject in a few days.

Knit front and back (KFB) is a bar increase (one that creates a bar resembling a purl stitch) and is very easy to do. This increase is very visible on stockinette stitch and practically disappears on garter stitch.

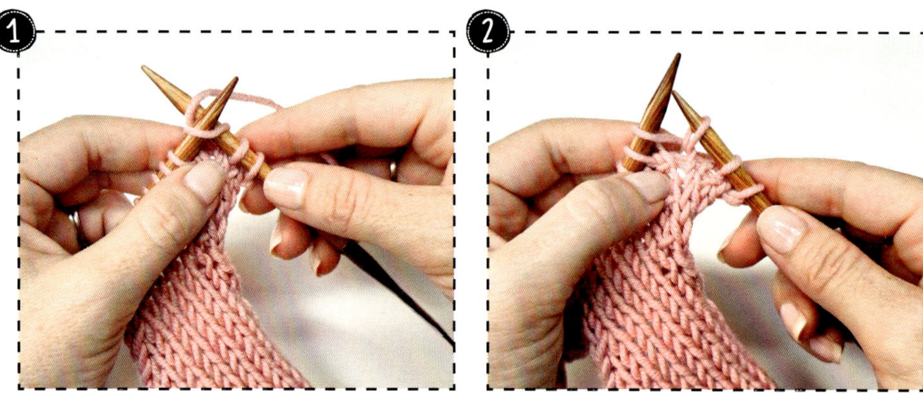

Knit one without dropping the stitch from the left needle.

Insert your right needle through the back loop of the same stitch and again knit one. Drop the stitch from the left needle. You have knit 2 stitches into one, thus creating a new stitch.

The least conspicuous increase is called **Make 1 Left (M1L)**. If you're ever unsure, you can almost always use this type of increase if the pattern doesn't call for a specific one. It is knit between 2 stitches, generally on the right side of your work.

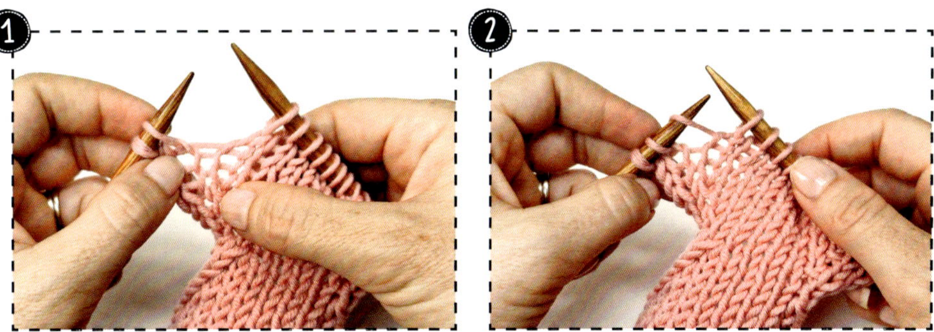

With the left needle, take up the horizontal strand found between 2 stitches, from front to back.

Insert the right needle through the back loop of the yarn and knit one. You now have an additional stitch on your needles and you can see the crossed loop under the needle where you have created this new stitch.

Lesson

THE RIB STITCH

To make 1 × 1 rib stitch, alternate one knit and one purl along an entire row. To do this, you need to make sure you're placing the yarn on the correct side of your work for each stitch, or you will inadvertently add stitches. Here is the rhythm for 1 × 1 ribs:

1

Knit the first stitch. Bring the yarn forward between the 2 needles.

2

Purl the next stitch. Put the yarn back, passing between the 2 needles, and knit the following stitch. Repeat these steps until you reach the end of the row.

Keep in mind: If you have an even number of stitches and you started your first row with a knit stitch, you will start all following rows with a knit stitch. If you have an odd number of stitches, you will need to make sure you're using the right stitch to achieve the 1 × 1 rib. Remember that a knit stitch creates a V and a purl stitch creates a wave. Look directly below the stitch on the needle to figure out which stitch to make.

Ribs can be made in various forms: 2 × 2, 3 × 3, 2 × 1, 3 × 1, etc. The numbers always refer to knits first and purls second.

Tip: If you finish a row with a purl stitch, start the next row with a knit stitch.

If you finish a row with a knit, start the next row with a purl.

TODAY'S PRACTICE

On your practice piece, knit a few rows of 1 × 1 rib to get a feel for the rhythm. As you work, you may forget to put the yarn forward or back before making a stitch. If this happens, you will see a strand on your needle connecting 2 stitches. Congratulations—you have stumbled upon the yarn over, which we will discuss on Day 18. Since you don't need this yet, you should simply drop this thread from your needle when you reach it on the next row.

Lesson START FINGERLESS GLOVES

MATERIALS

- Size 10 needles (6mm)
- 1 ball of bulky or worsted merino yarn (Teal)
- Yarn needle and scissors
- 2 stitch markers
- A piece of yarn

SKILLS

- Casting on
- Knit stitch
- Purl stitch
- Make 1 Left increases
- Binding off

STEP-BY-STEP

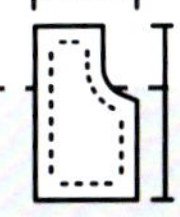

PATTERN / Ribs

R 1 = Cast on 30 sts.
R 2–10 = *k1, p1* until the end of the row.

PATTERN / Thumb panel

R 1: k
R 2 and all following even-numbered rows: p
R 3: k14, pm, M1L, k2, M1L, pm, k14 (increase of 2 sts)
R 5: k until m, sm, M1L, k until m, M1L, sm, k until end (increase of 2 sts)
Repeat, alternating row 5 and the purled row until you have 12 stitches between the markers. These stitches will form the thumb. Stop after a purled row.
Dividing row: k until m, remove the marker, put the stitches of the thumb on hold on a piece of yarn using your yarn needle. Cast on 2 stitches using a simple cast-on (photos 1, 2, 3) and k until the end of the row

1

2

3

PATTERN / Hand

R 1 (WS): p every stitch
R 2 (RS): k every stitch
R 3–7: alternate rows 1 and 2 (finishing with a p row)

PATTERN / Ribs

R 1–6: *k1, p1* until the end of the row
Bind off. Cut the yarn to a length 2 times the height of the glove to use for sewing.

Project FINISH

FINGERLESS GLOVES

PATTERN / Thumb

Take back up the stitches on hold for the thumb and start knitting on the right side of the work

R 1–4: *k1, p1* until the end of the row.

Bind off. Cut the yarn to a length 2 times the height of the thumb to use for sewing.

Knit a second fingerless glove following the same instructions. Wash and block (see Tips and Tricks, page 76). Tomorrow you'll sew the gloves.

Project SEW FINGERLESS GLOVES

To finish your gloves, you will need to make 2 seams: one for the hand and one for the thumb. Now is the time to learn this method of invisible sewing: the ladder stitch.

Fold the glove in half to line up the edges. Position it so that you have the seam horizontal and the yarn tail to the right.

Thread the yarn needle. Find the row of Vs closest to the edge (you may have to unroll the edge a bit to find it).

Pass the needle under the first 2 vertical bars after the row of Vs on the back piece.

Pass the needle under the first 2 vertical bars after the row of Vs on the front piece.

Insert the needle where you came out of the back piece, and pass it under 2 vertical bars. Then, insert the needle where you came out of the front piece and pass it under 2 vertical bars. Alternate these 2 steps until the end.

Use the same technique for the thumb. Then use the yarn to close the hole at the junction of the thumb.

Note: The most important thing in achieving an invisible seam is to follow the same column of stitches. If you are not happy with the result, don't hesitate to undo the seam and start over!

Lesson KNIT IN THE ROUND

To knit in the round, you will need circular knitting needles with the same circumference as your project or shorter. Since the circular-knit project in this book is a beanie, you will use cables that are 16″ (40cm) or less.

To understand knitting in the round, you simply need to know that you will always be knitting on the right side of your work (unlike flat knitting where you work one row on the right side then one row on the wrong side).

Any flat design can be done in the round, you just need to think about the result you want on the right side of the work.

EXAMPLES

GARTER STITCH KNIT FLAT
R 1 (RS)–knit
R 2 (WS)–knit

GARTER STITCH IN THE ROUND
R 1 (RS)–knit
R 2 (RS)–purl

STOCKINETTE STITCH KNIT FLAT
R 1–knit
R 2–purl

STOCKINETTE STITCH IN THE ROUND
R 1–knit
R 2–knit

JOINING IN THE ROUND

To successfully knit in the round, you must pay particular attention to the first stitch when you join. If you add a twist when you join the beginning and end of a row, it will be impossible to knit a tube and you will need to start over. You can join your circular knitting from the first row, but for your first attempts, I recommend turning as you would for flat knitting before joining. This way, it will be easier to see if your work is properly lined up.

TODAY'S PRACTICE

Cast on 64 stitches, knit one row and back again in whichever stitch you prefer (2 × 2 ribs in the photo). After the second row, don't turn the work.

Form a circle with your needles, with the last stitch you knit on the right. Position the knitting, making sure that the cast-on row is on the inside of the circle without ever twisting around the cable.

✔

✘

Take up your needles and resume working in the first stitch on the left needle.

Continue to knit following your pattern, always in the same direction, never turning the work.

Note: It is normal for a visible space to appear at the join. You can use the yarn tail from the beginning and a yarn needle to tighten everything up at the end.

CHANGING SKEINS
OR COLORS IN THE ROUND

When you're knitting in the round and need to add a new ball of yarn, you can simply drop the remaining yarn and start up with the new yarn. Yes, there will be a hole, but it will be closed after you've woven your thread tails at the end. Just like changing skeins when knitting flat, you can tie a loose knot with the 2 yarn tails to prevent the hole from getting bigger as you knit.

If you're knitting stripes, it is completely normal for the stripes not to line up perfectly at the beginning of the row since circular knitting is actually an infinite spiral and not a series of circles stacked on top of each other. Make sure you make this color change somewhere less visible, like the side on a sweater or the back on a hat or neck warmer.

When making thin stripes (4 rows or less), you can continue with each yarn without cutting, as you would for flat knitting. The trick for making the join as pretty as possible is to take the color that you just finished with and place it above and to the left of the color you're taking up, as shown in the photo.

START

CIRCULAR-KNIT BEANIE

MATERIALS

- Size 10 circular needles (6mm), 16″ (40cm) cable or shorter
- 3 balls of bulky or worsted merino yarn Color A—Blue, Color B—Ecru, Color C—Teal)
- Yarn needle and scissors

SKILLS

- Casting on
- Knit stitch
- Purl stitch
- Joining in the round
- Decreasing
- Changing color

I recommend starting by first making a beanie in a single color to practice your circular knitting. In that case, ignore any mention of colors and the chart in the instructions.

Note for the grid: The color C yarn is never cut, colors A and B are only cut after working the 2 sections of 4 rows.

PATTERN / Border

R 1: With color A, cast on 64 stitches.
R 2–3 (flat): *k2, p2* until the end of the row
Do not turn the work after row 3 and pm at the beginning of the row, join in the round
R 4–10: *k2, p2* until the end of the row

PATTERN / Body

R 11–44: k (following the color chart if desired)

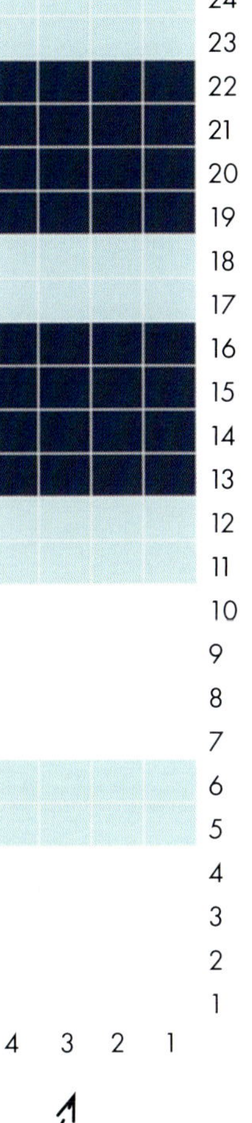

How to read the grid: Each square represents 1 stitch. It is read from right to left and from the bottom up. The numbers at the bottom indicate the stitches, the numbers on the right indicate the beginning of the row. Thus the grid for this pattern tells you which color to use for each row.

Grids are a visual way of explaining more complex stitching, such as openwork, cable knits, and jacquard patterns.

Project FINISH

CIRCULAR-KNIT BEANIE

PATTERN / Decreases

R 45: *k6, k2tog* until the end
R 46: k every stitch
(If you're using the chart, continue with color A until the end)
R 47: *k5, k2tog* until the end
R 48: k
R 49: *k4, k2tog* until the end
R 50: k
R 51: *k3, k2tog* until the end
R 52: k
R 53: *k2, k2tog* until the end
R 54: k2tog until the end of the row

Note: When your beanie is too small to continue knitting in the round, pull on the right needle to put the stitches entirely on the cable and left needle, then continue to knit. You can do this maneuver as many times as necessary to finish the decreases.

FINISHING

- Cut the yarn, leaving 4″ (10cm).
- Using your yarn needle, run the yarn through each stitch and pull to close the hole.
- Pull the yarn to the inside of the beanie through the middle of the hole. Run the yarn through each stitch a second time to prevent the hole from opening when worn.
- Weave in the yarn tails, and wash your beanie (see Tips and Tricks, page 76).

Lesson THE YARN OVER

The yarn over is an easy but visible way to add a stitch and is often paired with decreases to create both simple and more complex lacy textures.

DOING A YARN OVER ON A ROW OF KNIT STITCHES

Bring the yarn forward between the 2 needles (1), then knit the next stitch, letting the yarn pass over the right needle (2 and 3).

1

2

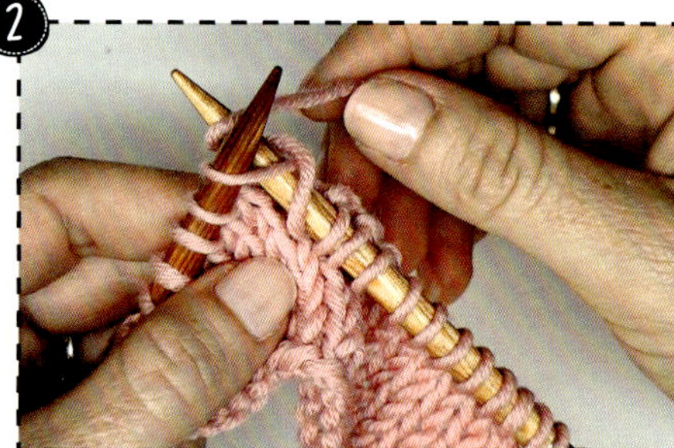

3

DOING A YARN OVER ON A ROW OF PURL STITCHES

Pull the yarn back over the right needle and bring it forward between the needles (1), then purl the next stitch (2).

1

2

WORKING IN A YARN OVER

Knit or purl in the front loop of the yarn over, as you would for a normal stitch.

WORKING IN A YARN OVER WITHOUT CREATING A HOLE

Knit or purl in the back loop of the yarn over. This will close the hole and the result will be similar to a simple increase.

Note: If you have forgotten to do a yarn over in the previous row, you can simply work until the spot where the yarn over should be and put the horizontal strand between the 2 stitches onto your left needle, inserting from front to back. The hole created will be slightly smaller than the others, but after washing and blocking, it won't stand out.

OTHER STITCHES

Here is a list of well-known stitches so you can experiment with possible patterns using the techniques you've learned over the past weeks. Have fun knitting squares to make decorative coasters or to join together to make a scarf, blanket, etc.

THE REVERSE RIDGE STITCH

Alternating knit stockinette and purl stockinette.

PATTERN / Flat, repeat these 6 rows

R 1 (RS): k
R 2 (WS): p
R 3: k
R 4: k
R 5: p
R 6: k

PATTERN / Round, repeat these 6 rows

R 1–3: k
R 4–6: p

THE SEED STITCH

Alternating knits and purls, reversed on each row: purl the knits (the stitches that look like little Vs) and knit the purls (stitches that look like waves). The seed stitch is worked the same way both flat and in the round (repeat the 2 rows, and use an even number of stitches when working in the round).

PATTERN

R 1: *k1, p1* until the end of the row
R 2: Reverse your stitches

THE MOSS STITCH

Alternating knits and purls, reversed every 2 rows.

It is worked the same way both flat and in the round (repeat the 4 rows, and use an even number of stitches when working in the round).

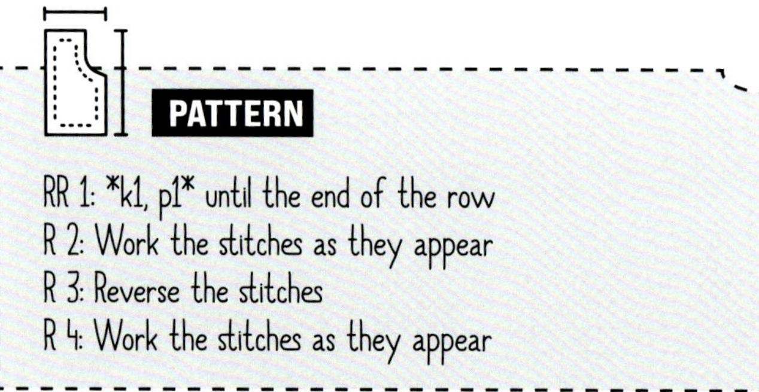

PATTERN

RR 1: *k1, p1* until the end of the row
R 2: Work the stitches as they appear
R 3: Reverse the stitches
R 4: Work the stitches as they appear

THE BROKEN RIB STITCH

When reversed, this becomes the sand stitch. Alternating columns of stockinette and garter stitches.

This is worked the same way both flat and in the round (repeat the 2 rows, and use an even number of stitches when working in the round).

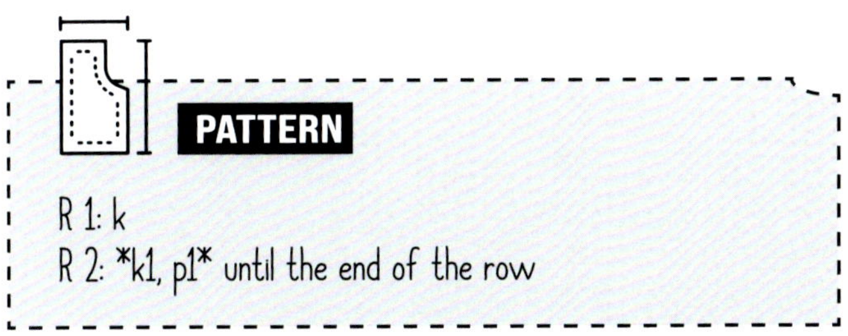

PATTERN

R 1: k
R 2: *k1, p1* until the end of the row

THE MOCK CABLE STITCH

Also called the coffee bean stitch or the eyelet mock cable stitch.

PATTERN / Flat, repeat rows 1 to 4, worked on a multiple of 5 stitches

Preparation row (WS): *k3, p2*
R 1: *k1, yarn over (yo), k1, p3* until the end of the row
R 2: *k3, p3* until the end of the row
R 3: *k3, pass the 3rd st on the right needle over the first 2 as if binding off, p3* until the end of the row
R 4: *k3, p2* until the end of the row

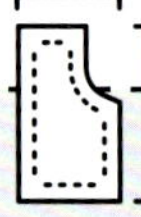

PATTERN / Round, repeat rows 1 to 4

R 1: *k2, p3* until the end of the row
R 2: *k1, yo, k1, p3* until the end of the row
R 3: *k3, p3* until the end of the row
R 4: *k3, pass the 3rd st on the right needle over the first 2 as if binding off, p3* until the end of the row

Project NECK WARMER

MATERIALS

- Size 10 circular needles, 16″ (40cm) cable or shorter
- 1 ball of bulky or worsted merino yarn (Pale peach)
- Yarn needle and scissors

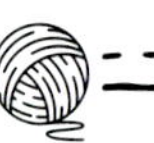

SKILLS

- Casting on
- Knitting and purling
- Joining in the round
- Mock cable stitch
- Make 1 Left (M1L) increases
- Binding off

With what you've learned over the last few days, you can personalize this neck warmer to suit your tastes. You can start out with ribs, switch to any of the stitches learned on Day 18, then change back to ribs to finish the project. My version includes staggered rows of mock cables and increases for a flared effect at the base of the neck.

PATTERN / 2 × 3 ribbed section

R 1: Cast on 80 stitches and knit in the round
R 2–7: *k2, p3* until the end of the row

PATTERN / S2 × 3 ribbed section (mock cable)

R 1: *k1, yo, k1, p3, k2, p3* until the end of the row
R 2: *k3, p3, k2, p3* until the end of the row
R 3: *k3, pass the 3rd st on the right needle over the first 2 as if binding off, p3, k2, p3* until the end of the row
R 4: *k2, p3* until the end of the row
R 5: *k2, p3, k1, yo, k1, p3* until the end of the row
R 6: *k2, p3, k3, p3* until the end of the row
R 7: *k2, p3, k3, pass the 3rd st on the right needle over the first 2 as if binding off, p3* until the end of the row
R 8: *k2, p3* until the end of the row
Repeat rows 1–8 two more times.

PATTERN / Flared section

R 1: *k1, yo, k1, p3, k1, M1L, k1, p3* until the end of the row
R 2: *k3, p3* until the end of the row
R 3: *k3, pass the 3rd st on the right needle over the first 2 as if binding off, p3, k3, p3* until the end of the row
R 4–5: *k2, p3, k3, p3* until the end of the row
R 6: *k1, M1L, k1, p3, k3, p3* until the end of the row
R 7–10: *k3, p3* until the end of the row
Bind off

Lesson MAKING A GAUGE SWATCH

When you choose a pattern, you will see a note about a gauge swatch or tension square. What is that? Why do you need one? A gauge swatch is a square you will need to knit with the recommended needles and your chosen yarn to analyze the result. Making a gauge swatch allows you to verify that your knitting conforms to the specifications provided by the pattern, as much for the tension as for the finish and fit of your knitting. You can then change which needles you'll use (or the yarn, if necessary). When you start to make garments, achieving the recommended gauge is crucial to have both the intended size and finish.

MAKING A GAUGE SWATCH

Cast on at least the number of stitches recommended for 6″ (15cm) of knitting (e.g., if the recommended gauge is 20 stitches for 4″ or 10cm, cast on 30 stitches).

Knit the stitch required for the swatch until you have a square.

Wash and let dry in the same way you would for your finished work.

MEASURING THE GAUGE

Use a ruler to measure 4″ (10cm) in width and height in the middle of your swatch (do not measure along the edges since these stitches are not always the same size)

and mark these 4″ with pins. Count the Vs between the pins. You also need to count partial stitches. If you're missing half a stitch in 4″ (10cm), a cardigan that should be 60″ (150cm) in circumference will be larger than intended. You can now understand the importance of a good gauge swatch, as it will determine the result of your work.

If you have too many stitches and rows: this means that you knit too tightly or the yarn is too thin, so try a larger sized needle.

If you have too few stitches or rows: this means you knit too loosely or the yarn is too thick, so try a smaller sized needle.

Don't hesitate to knit as many gauge swatches as you need. You can compare them before making your decision as to the size of needles you'll use. You are not wasting time or yarn; it's better to knit several swatches to be sure of the gauge than to end up with work that is too big or too small. If you don't have enough yarn to finish your project, undo your gauge swatches.

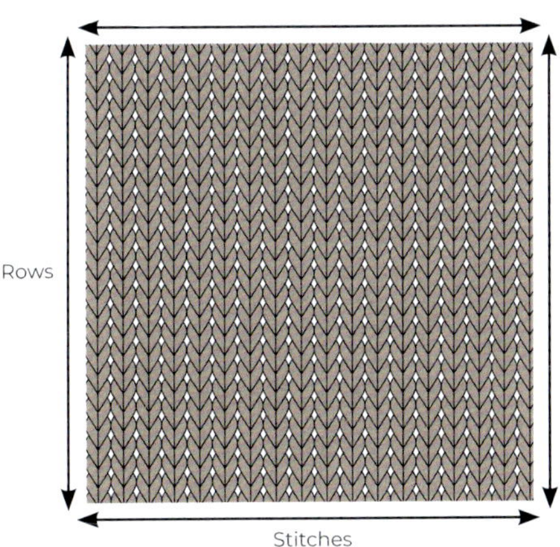

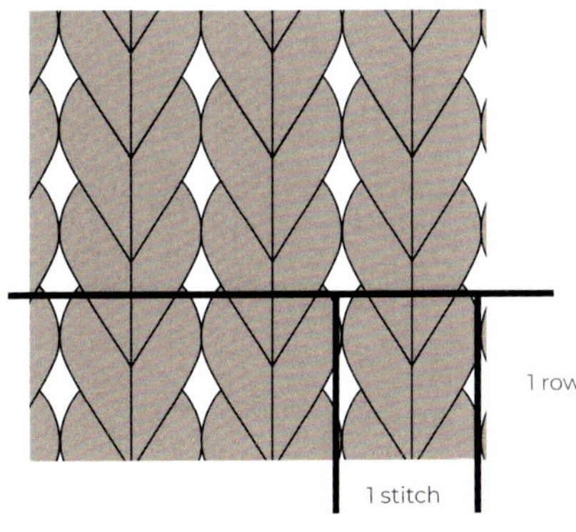

Project TRIANGULAR SHAWL

MATERIALS

- Size 6 circular needles (4mm), 24″ (60cm) or shorter
- 3 balls of fine merino yarn (Teal, Pale peach, and Blue)
- Yarn needle and scissors

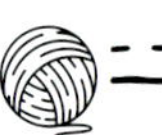

SKILLS

- Casting on
- Knitting and purling
- Yarn over
- Decreasing
- Increasing
- Binding off

This shawl can be knit in one or several colors, so have fun choosing your color palette. Just make sure you have at least 425 yards (390m) of yarn in total. For this project, I've opted for needles with a larger size than is recommended for this yarn to achieve a more fluid result. You can also use size 5 needles (3.5mm) for a slightly denser result.

PATTERN / Casting on and foundation with color A

RR 1: Cast on 5 stitches
R 2 (WS): k
R 3 (RS): k
R 4: k2, yo, k1, yo, k2 (7 stitches)
R 5: k
R 6: k2, yo, p1, pm, p1, pm, yo, p1, k2 (9 stitches)

PATTERN / Section 1, stockinette with color A

R 1 (RS): k2, yo, k until m, yo, sm, k1, sm, yo, k until 2 stitches from the end, yo, k2 (increase of 4 stitches)
R 2 (WS): k2, yo, p until 2 stitches from the end, yo, k2 (increase of 2 stitches)

Repeat rows 1 and 2 three more times. You now have 33 stitches on your needles.

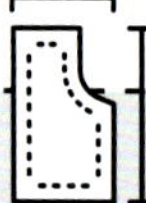

PATTERN / Section 2, stripes with colors A and B

Add color B without cutting color A.
Do rows 1 and 2 of section 1 with color B.
Do rows 1 and 2 of section 1 with color A.
Repeat these 4 rows three more times. Cut the color A yarn.

You now have 81 stitches on your needles.

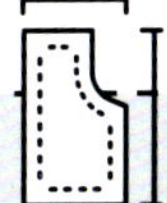

PATTERN / Section 3, garter stitch with color B

R 1: k2, yo, k until m, yo, sm, k1, sm, yo, k until 2 stitches from the end, yo, k2 (increase of 4 stitches)
R 2: k2, yo, k until m, p1, k until 2 stitches from the end, yo, k2 (increase of 2 stitches)

Repeat these 2 rows seven more times. Cut color B. You now have 129 stitches on your needles.

PATTERN / Section 4, eyelets with color C

R 1: k2, yo, pm, *k8, yo, k2tog* until 2 stitches from m, place another marker, k2, yo, sm, k1, sm, yo, k2, pm, *ssk, yo, k8* until 2 stitches from the end, pm, yo, k2 (increase of 4 stitches)
R 2 (and every even row): k2, yo, p until 2 stitches from the end, yo, k2 (increase of 2 stitches)
R 3: k2, yo, k until m, *k8, yo, k2tog* until m, k until m, yo, sm, k1, sm, yo, k until m, *ssk, yo, k8* until m, sm, k until 2 stitches from the end, yo, k2 (increase of 4 stitches)
Repeat rows 2 and 3 six more times

You now have 177 stitches on your needles. You can remove all markers in the next row, except the two in the middle.

Note: The eyelet repetitions are done every 10 stitches. The increases on each side and in the center of your knitting are always knits on the right side and purls on the wrong side. The markers placed on row 1 of this section indicate when to start and finish your repetitions.

PATTERN / Section 5, stripes with colors C and A

Add color A without cutting color C.

Do rows 1 and 2 of section 1 with color A.

Do rows 1 and 2 of section 1 with color C.

Repeat these 4 rows four more times. Cut color C.

You now have 237 stitches on your needles.

PATTERN / Section 6, garter stitch with color A

Do rows 1 and 2 of section 3 a total of eight times.

You now have 285 stitches on your needles.

PATTERN / Section 7, eyelets with color B

1: k2, yo, pm, *k8, yo, k2tog* until m, sm, yo, place another marker, k1, sm, yo, place another marker, *ssk, yo, k8* until 2 stitches from the end, pm, yo, k2 (increase of 4 stitches)
R 2 (and every even row): k2, yo, p until 2 stitches from the end, yo, k2 (increase of 2 stitches)
R 3: k2, yo, k until m, *k8, yo, k2tog* until m, k until m, yo, sm, k1, sm, yo, k until m, *ssk, yo, k8* until m, sm, k until 2 stitches from the end, yo, k2 (increase of 4 stitches)
Repeat rows 2 and 3 six more times

You now have 333 stitches on your needles and you can remove all the markers in the next row, except the 2 in the middle.

PATTERN / Section 8, 4 × 4 ribs with color C

R 1: k2, yo, *k4, p4* until m, yo, sm, k1, sm, yo, *p4, k4* until 2 stitches from the end, yo, k2
R 2: k2, yo, k1, *p4, k4* until m, sm, p1, sm, p1, *k4, p4* until 2 stitches from the end, yo, k2
Repeat rows 1 and 2 three more times, following the pattern for the added stitches.
Bind off following the pattern (knit the knits and purls the purls).
Wash and block (see Tips and Tricks, page 76).

Depending on your chosen yarn, you may or may not be able to put your knitting in the dryer. In any case, I recommend stretching it on a flat surface to block it; this way it will spread out completely, the openwork will be revealed, and the shawl will drape beautifully.

Note: When you knit the yarn-overs, look at your ribs to see if you need to do a knit or a purl in order to continue the pattern.

TIPS AND TRICKS

COUNTING STITCHES AND ROWS

1. On stockinette: It's simple, you just need to count the Vs horizontally and vertically.

2. On garter stitch: Horizontally, count the waves. Vertically, you have alternating Vs and waves every two rows. Count the waves and multiply by two.

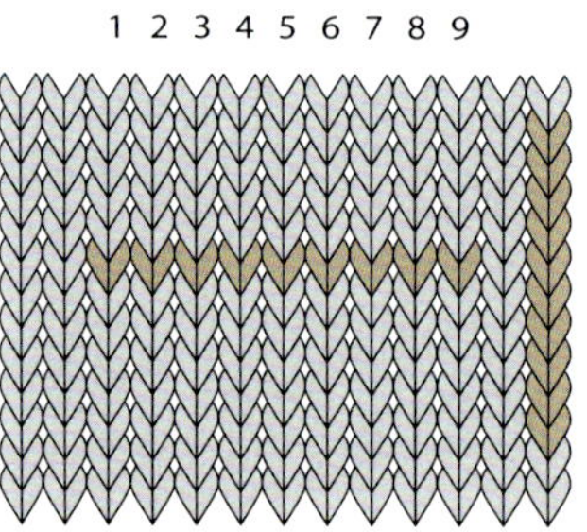

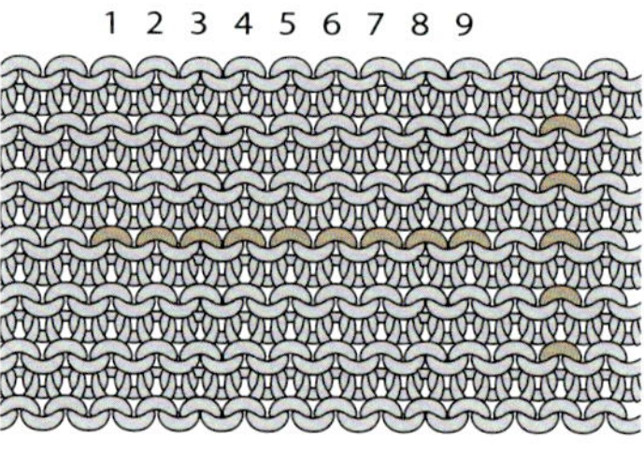

WORKING STITCHES AS THEY APPEAR

To work stitches as they appear: if you see a V on the row under the needle, knit. If you see a bridge, purl.

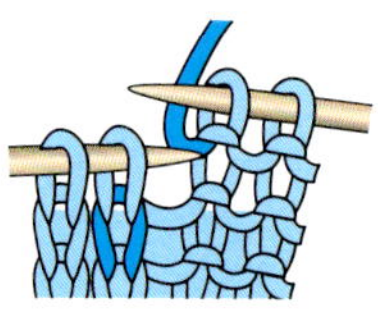

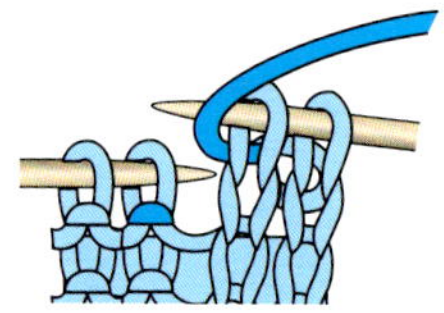

REVERSING YOUR STITCHES

If you see a V on the row under the needle, purl. If you see a bridge, knit.

Keep in mind: Don't forget to move your yarn behind the needle to do a knit stitch and bring it forward to do a purl stitch.

UNDOING A STITCH

When you notice a mistake in the same row, you can go back, undoing one stitch at a time until you reach the mistake. To do this, insert the left needle from front to back in the middle of the stitch under the right needle and drop the stitch from the right needle to undo it.

UNDOING A KNIT

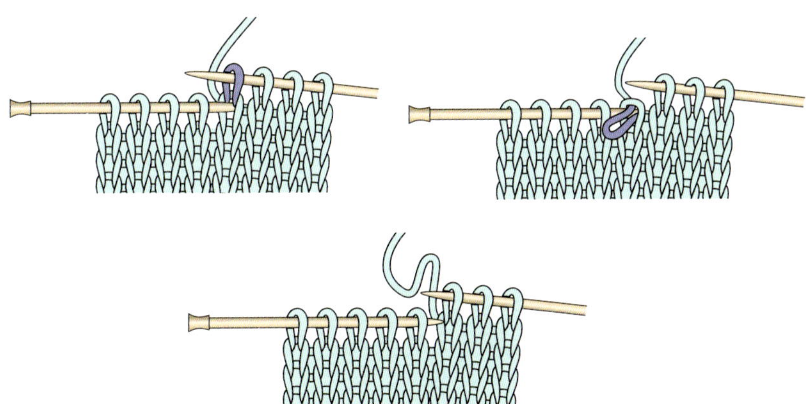

UNDOING A PURL

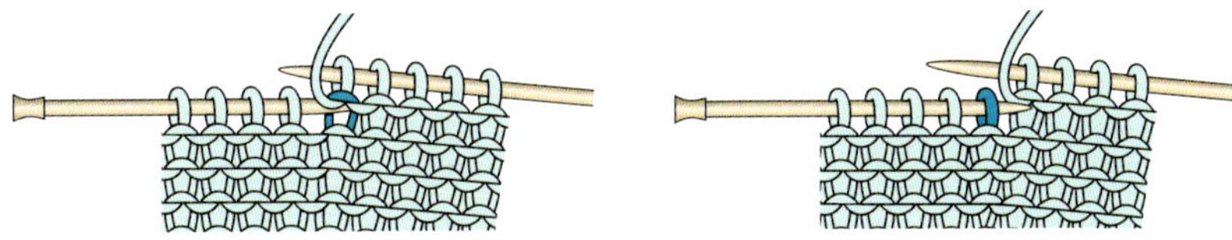

DROPPED STITCHES

I've dropped a stitch off the needle. What do I do? First off, don't panic! Locate the loop you need to secure and put it on a pin, a crochet hook, or a needle before you analyze the situation. If you see one or several strands connecting the columns to the left and right of the dropped stitch, you will need to remake the stitches with a crochet hook as illustrated here:

ON GARTER

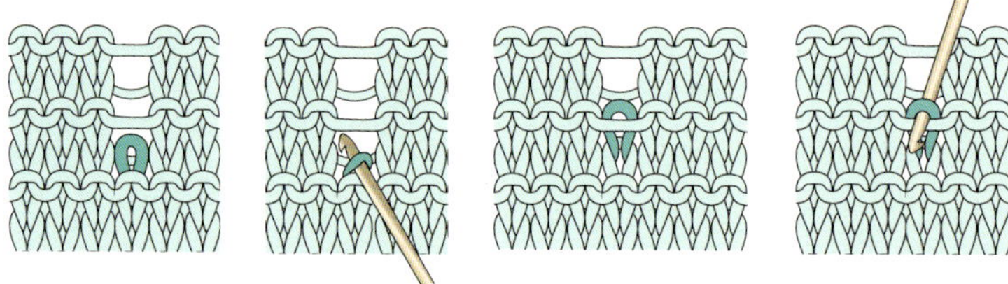

ON STOCKINETTE

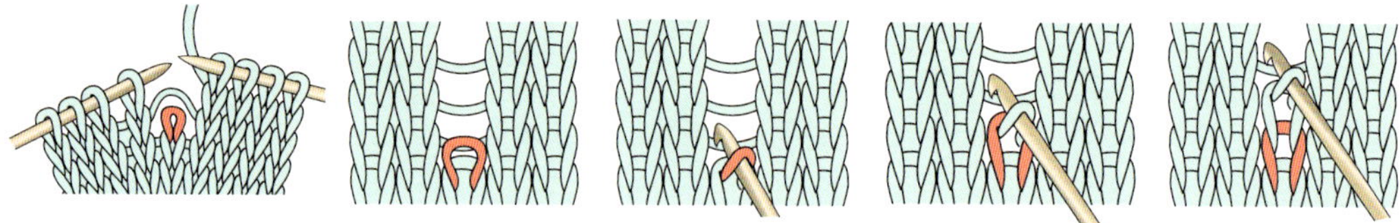

Important: It is very important to put the stitch on your needle in the right direction, or else you will have a twisted stitch in your work. When we look at the stitches on the left needle, the front loop comes before the back loop. If you have twisted your stitch when picking it back up, turn it around to put it in the right direction when you place it on your needle.

✔

✘

Tip: You can also use your knitting needles to remake stitches if you don't have a crochet hook. Insert the needle like in the illustration and use the other needle or your fingers to pass the stitch over the strand and the tip of the needle to raise the dropped stitch.

I'VE KNIT THE WRONG STITCH

If you see a knit where a purl should be or a purl where a knit should be, you can drop it from your needle and undo it, then later redo it as shown in the section on dropped stitches. Ideally, you should always check your needles frequently for these little mistakes to catch them as quickly as possible, which makes fixing them less complicated.

WEAVING IN YARN TAILS

When you finish a project, you need to weave in the yarn tails that come out of your work. Generally, there are at least two, one from casting on and one from binding off. There will also be yarn tails from color changes or the ends of skeins if the pattern calls for it.

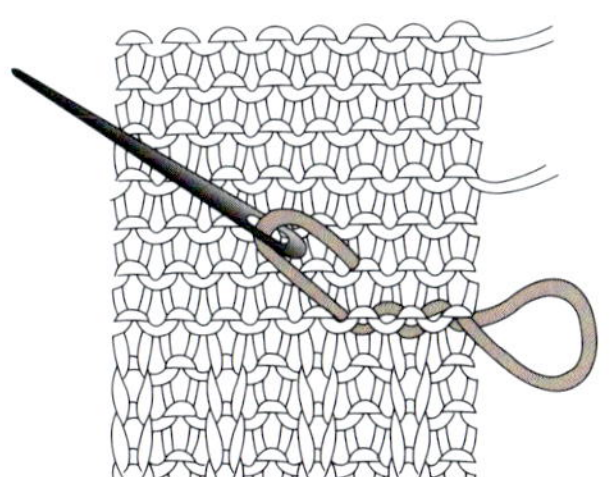

- Thread a yarn needle.
- On the wrong side, run your yarn through the work, forming a sort of wave through the stitches in a row for at least 2″ (5cm) as shown in the drawing.
- Cut the yarn, leaving a little extra since it will move a little during washing.

WASHING AND BLOCKING YOUR KNITS

Just like any other fabric, your knits will reveal their full beauty once washed.

- If you're using a fiber other than wool, see the label for the manufacturer's washing and drying recommendations.

- If you're using wool, it may be designated superwash which makes it less prone to felting. You can put superwash wool yarn in the washing machine on a delicate or wool cycle. You can also put it in the dryer on a low temperature if you want.

- If the yarn is not treated, you will need to gently handwash your piece (never put untreated wool in the machine). Simply soak your knitting in warm to hot water with a gentle soap for at least 15 minutes. Be sure not to scrub it too much, as it's the combination of scrubbing and the water's heat that causes felting. After soaking, rinse your knit if your soap requires it, then remove as much water as possible by rolling and pressing it in a towel. Above all, do not wring out your knitting!

- If you're using a natural fiber like wool or cotton, it is also important to block your work. Blocking is the process of drying your project in its intended final shape. This is often as simple as laying the knit flat, making sure it's in the right shape. Wool is a fiber with memory, so you need to block it like this every time you wash your knitting.

BONUS WORKBOOK

BASIC STITCHES, RIBS, AND TEXTURES FOR GOING FURTHER

THE GARTER STITCH

With two needles:

Always knit or always purl. The wrong side of the work looks just like the right side.

Our advice: remember when counting your rows, on the wrong side and on the right side, there is always 1 row sunk in alternating with 1 row sticking out.

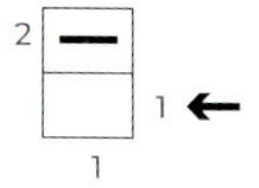

THE STOCKINETTE STITCH

With two needles:

1st row (right side of the work): knit every stitch.

2nd row: purl every stitch.

Repeat these 2 rows.

With four needles: knit every stitch.

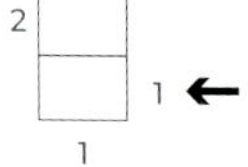

- knit stitch on the right side or purl stitch on the wrong side
- purl stitch on the right side or knit stitch on the wrong side
- slip stitch purlwise on the right side (with yarn in back) or purlwise on the wrong side (with yarn in front)
- 2 stitches together on the right side
- twisted knit stitch on the right side or twisted purl stitch on the wrong side
- twisted purl stitch on the right side or twisted knit stitch on the wrong side
- slip stitch purlwise on the right side (with yarn in front) or purlwise on the wrong side (with yarn in back)
- yarn over

THE HALF LINEN STITCH

Number of stitches for symmetry: multiple of 2 + 1 + 1 edge stitch on each side.

1st row (right side of work): 1 edge stitch, *knit 1, slip 1 purlwise (with yarn in front)*; repeat from * to *; finish with 1 knit, 1 edge stitch.

2nd and 4th rows: purl every stitch.

3rd row: 1 edge stitch, *slip 1 purlwise (with yarn in front), knit 1*; repeat from * to *; finish with 1 slipped stitch purlwise (with yarn in front), 1 edge stitch.

Repeat these 4 rows.

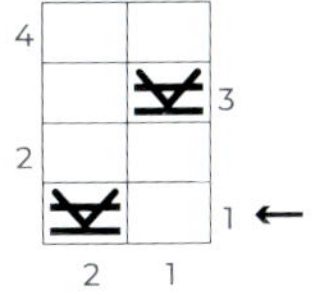

THE LINEN STITCH

Number of stitches for symmetry: multiple of 2 + 1 + 1 edge stitch on each side.

1st row (right side of work): 1 edge stitch, *knit 1, slip 1 purlwise (with yarn in front)*; repeat from * to *; finish with 1 knit, 1 edge stitch.

2nd row: 11 edge stitch, slip 1 purlwise (with yarn in back), *purl 1, slip 1 purlwise (with yarn in back)*; repeat from * to *; finish with 1 edge stitch.

Repeat these 2 rows.

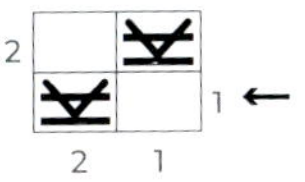

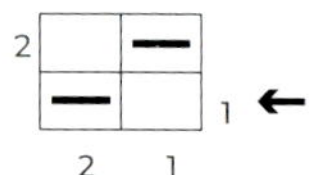

THE SEED STITCH

Number of stitches for symmetry: multiple of 2 + 1 + 1 edge stitch on each side.

1st row (right side of work): 1 edge stitch, *knit 1, purl 1*; repeat from * to *; finish with 1 knit, 1 edge stitch.

2nd row: like the first row.

Repeat these 2 rows.

The stitches are therefore reversed with each row. You knit the purls and purl the knits, the opposite of working stitches as they appear.

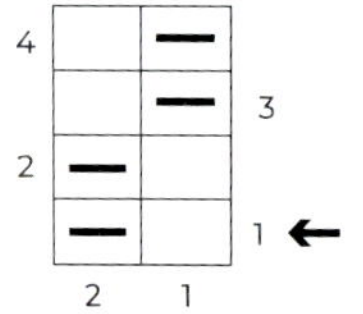

THE MOSS STITCH

Number of stitches for symmetry: multiple of 2 + 1 + 1 edge stitch on each side.

1st row (right side of work): 1 edge stitch, *knit 1, purl 1*; repeat from * to *; finish with 1 knit, 1 edge stitch.

2nd and 4th rows: work the stitches as they appear.

3rd row: 1 edge stitch, *purl 1, knit 1*; repeat from * to *; finish with 1 purl, 1 edge stitch.

Repeat these 4 rows. The stitches are therefore reversed every other row.

THE REVERSE RIDGE STITCH

1st (right side of work), 3rd, 4th, and 6th rows: knit every stitch.

2nd and 5th rows: purl every stitch.

Repeat these 6 rows.

Our advice: very elastic, recommended for baby clothes.

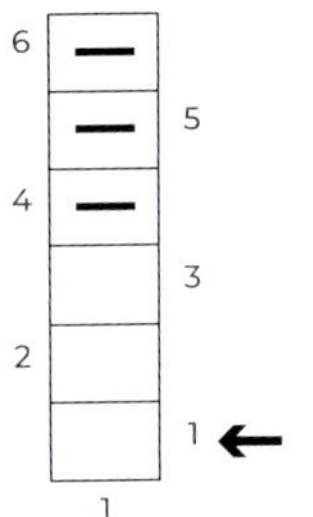

THE BROKEN RIB STITCH

Number of stitches for symmetry: multiple of 2 + 1 + 1 edge stitch on each side.

1st row (right side of work): knit every stitch.

2nd row: 1 edge stitch, purl 1, *knit 1, purl 1*; repeat from * to *; finish with 1 edge stitch.

Repeat these 2 rows.

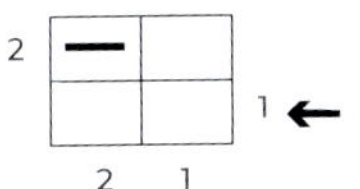

1 × 1 RIBS

Number of stitches for symmetry: multiple of 2 + 1 + 1 edge stitch on each side.

1st row (right side of work): 1 edge stitch, *knit 1, purl 1*; repeat from * to *; finish with 1 knit, 1 edge stitch.

2nd row and all following rows: work the stitches as they appear.

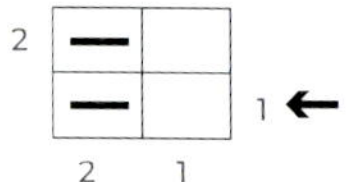

2 × 2 RIBS

Number of stitches for symmetry: multiple of 4 + 2 + 1 edge stitch on each side.

1st row (right side of work): 1 edge stitch, *knit 2, purl 2*; repeat from * to *; finish with 2 knits, 1 edge stitch.

2nd row and all following rows: work the stitches as they appear.

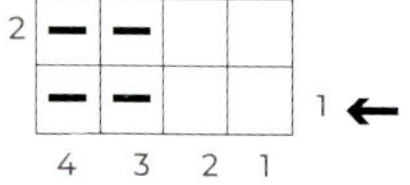

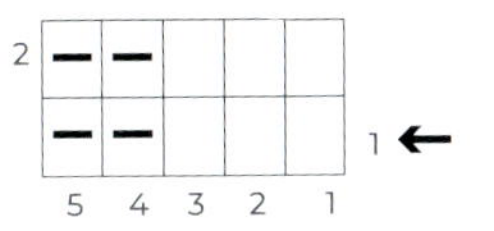

3 × 2 RIBS

Number of stitches for symmetry: multiple of 5 + 2 + 1 edge stitch on each side.

1st row (right side of work): 1 edge stitch, *purl 2, knit 3*; repeat from * to *; finish with 2 purls, 1 edge stitch.

2nd row and all following rows: work the stitches as they appear.

On the wrong side of the work, you have ribs of *knit 2, purl 3*.

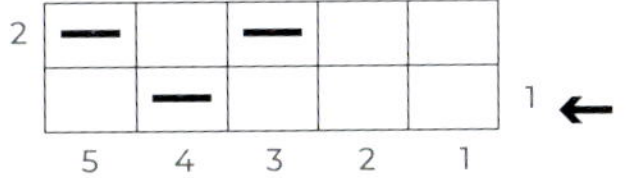

SEEDED RIBS

Number of stitches for symmetry: multiple of 5 + 2 + 1 edge stitch on each side.

1st row (right side of work): 1 edge stitch, *knit 3, purl 1, knit 1*; repeat from * to *; finish with 2 knits, 1 edge stitch.

2nd row: 1 edge stitch, purl 2, *knit 1, purl 1, knit 1 (so 3 stitches reversed), purl 2*; repeat from * to *; finish with 1 edge stitch.

Repeat these 2 rows.

THE SEERSUCKER STITCH

Number of stitches for symmetry: multiple of 4 + 1 + 1 edge stitch on each side.

1st (right side of work) and 5th rows: 1 edge stitch, *knit 1, purl 1, knit 1, purl 1*; repeat from * to *; finish with 1 knit, 1 edge stitch.

2nd row and all even rows: work the stitches as they appear.

3rd row: 1 edge stitch, *purl 1, knit 3*; repeat from * to *; finish with 1 purl, 1 edge stitch.

7th row: 1 edge stitch, *knit 2, purl 1, knit 1*; repeat from * to *; finish with 1 knit, 1 edge stitch.

Repeat rows 1 to 8.

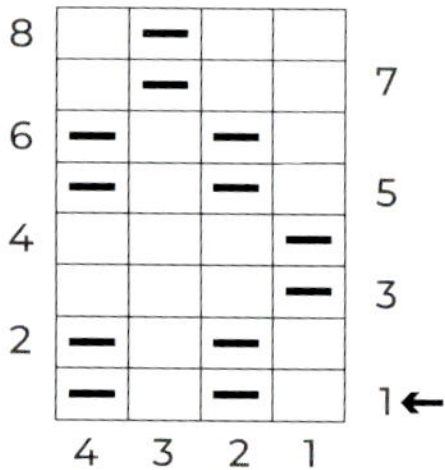

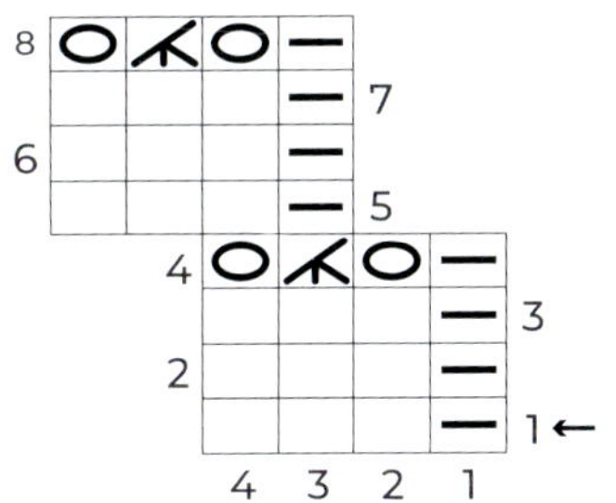

THE REVERSIBLE LAYETTE STITCH

Number of stitches for symmetry: multiple of 4 + 1 + 1 edge stitch on each side.

1st (right side of work) and 3rd rows: 1 edge stitch, *purl 1, knit 3*; repeat from * to *; finish with 1 purl, 1 edge stitch.

2nd and 6th rows: work the stitches as they appear.

4th row: 1 edge stitch, knit 1, *yarn over, purl 3 together, yarn over, knit 1*; repeat from * to *; finish with 1 edge stitch.

5th and 7th rows: 1 edge stitch, knit 2, *purl 1, knit 3*; repeat from * to *; finish with 1 purl, 2 knits, 1 edge stitch.

8th row: 1 edge stitch, purl 2 together, yarn over, knit 1, *yarn over, purl 3 together, yarn over, knit 1*; repeat from * to *; finish with 1 yarn over, purl 2 together, 1 edge stitch.

Repeat these 8 rows.

BRODERIE ANGLAISE

Number of stitches for symmetry: multiple of 8 + 4 + 1 edge stitch on each side.

Note: the stitch count from the beginning does not come back until row 4 is completed, then in rows 5, 8 (completed), and 9.

1st (wrong side of work), 3rd, 5th, 7th, and 9th rows: purl every stitch.

2nd row: 1 edge stitch, *knit 4, knit 2 together, slip-knit-pass over*; repeat from * to *; finish with 4 knits, 1 edge stitch.

4th row: 1 edge stitch, *knit 4, knit 1 long (insert the right needle 2 rows below, between the knit-2-together and the slip-knit-pass over, and knit 1, drawing up a loop), knit 2, knit 1 long (insert the right needle 2 rows below, between the knit-2-together and the slip-knit-pass over, and knit 1, drawing up a loop)*; repeat from * to *; finish with 4 knits, 1 edge stitch.

6th row: 1 edge stitch, *knit 2 together, slip-knit-pass over, knit 4*; repeat from * to *; finish with knit 2 together, slip-knit-pass over, 1 edge stitch.

8th row: 1 edge stitch, *knit 1 long as in row 4, knit 2, knit 1 long as in row 4*; repeat from * to *; finish with 1 long knit as in row 4, 2 knits, 1 long knit as in row 4, 1 edge stitch.

Repeat rows 2 to 9.

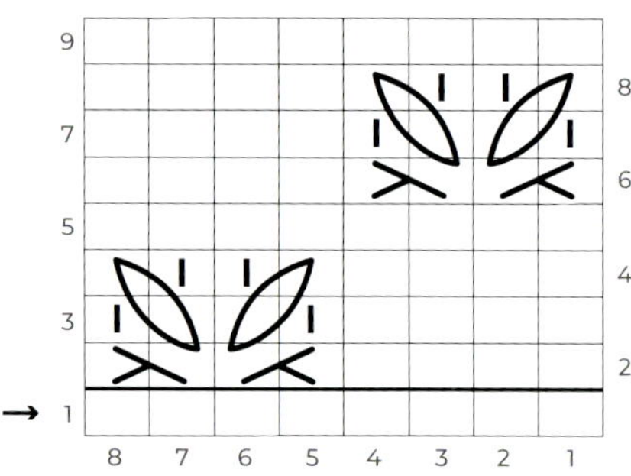

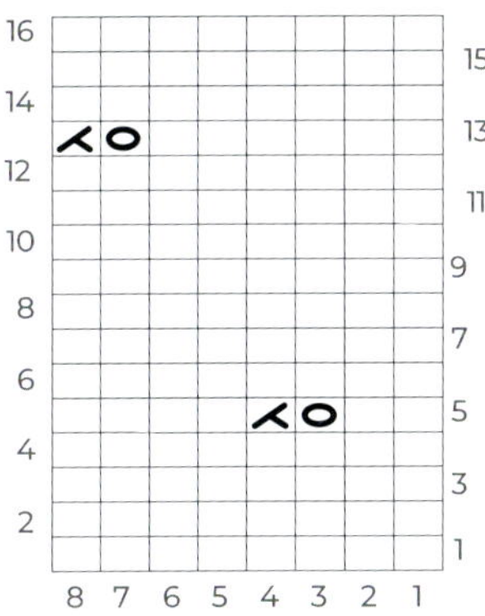

STAGGERED EYELETS

Number of stitches for continuity: multiple of 8 + 1 edge stitch on each side.

1st (right side of work), 3rd, 7th, 9th, 11th, and 15th rows: knit every stitch.

2nd row and all even rows: purl every stitch (and every yarn over).

5th row: 1 edge stitch, *knit 2, yarn over, knit 2 together, knit 4*; repeat from * to *; finish with 1 edge stitch.

13th row: 1 edge stitch, *knit 6, yarn over, knit 2 together*; repeat from * to *; finish with 1 edge stitch.

Repeat these 16 rows.

THE DIAMOND EYELET STITCH

Number of stitches for symmetry: multiple of 12 + 7 + 1 edge stitch on each side.

1st (right side of work) and 5th rows: 1 edge stitch, *knit 2, knit 2 together, yarn over, knit 8*; repeat from * to *; finish with: knit 2, knit 2 together, yarn over, knit 3, 1 edge stitch.

2nd row and all even rows: purl every stitch (and every yarn over).

3rd row: 1 edge stitch, *knit 1, knit 2 together, yarn over, knit 2 together, yarn over, knit 7*; repeat from * to *; finish with: knit 1, knit 2 together, yarn over, knit 2 together, yarn over, knit 2, 1 edge stitch.

7th and 15th rows: knit every stitch.

9th and 13th rows: 1 edge stitch, *knit 8, knit 2 together, yarn over, knit 2 together*; repeat from * to *; finish with 7 knits, 1 edge stitch.

11th row: 1 edge stitch, *knit 7, knit 2 together, yarn over, knit 2 together, yarn over, knit 1*; finish with 7 knits, 1 edge stitch.

Repeat these 16 rows.

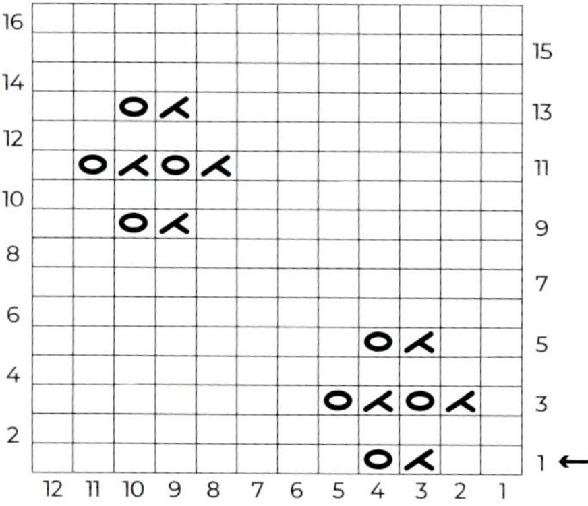

EYELET CHEVRONS

Number of stitches for symmetry: multiple of 16 + 1 + 1 edge stitch on each side.

1st row (right side of work): 1 edge stitch, *purl 1, yarn over, knit 2, knit 2 together, knit 7, slip-knit-pass over, knit 2, yarn over*; repeat * to *; finish with 1 purl, 1 edge stitch.

2nd row and all even rows: work the stitches as they appear and purl every yarn over.

3rd row: 1 edge stitch, *purl 1, knit 1, yarn over, knit 2, knit 2 together, knit 5, slip-knit-pass over, knit 2, yarn over, knit 1*; repeat from * to *; finish with 1 purl, 1 edge stitch.

5th row: 1 edge stitch, *purl 1, knit 2, yarn over, knit 2, knit 2 together, knit 3, slip-knit-pass over, knit 2, yarn over, knit 2*; repeat from * to *; finish with 1 purl, 1 edge stitch.

7th row: 1 edge stitch, *purl 1, knit 3, yarn over, knit 2, knit 2 together, knit 1, slip-knit-pass over, knit 2, yarn over, knit 3*; repeat from * to *; finish with 1 purl, 1 edge stitch.

9th row: 1 edge stitch, *purl 1, knit 4, yarn over, knit 2, slip 2-knit-pass over (centered double decrease: slip 2 stitches as if to knit 2 together, knit the 3rd stitch, pass the 2 slipped stitches over the new stitch), knit 2, yarn over, knit 4*; repeat from * to *; finish with 1 purl, 1 edge stitch.

Repeat these 10 rows.

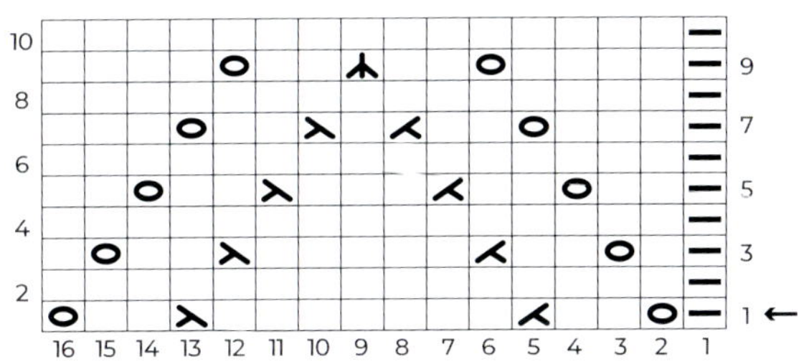

CHART
OF YARN WEIGHTS

Symbol	Category	Gauge/ 4″ (10cm)	Needles in US / metric	Wraps per inch (WPI)
0	Lace	33–40 st	000–1 / 1.5–2.25	30–40 and +
1	Fingering, sock	27–32 st	1–3 / 2.25–3.25	14–30
2	Sport, baby	23–26 st	3–5 / 3.25–3.75	12–18
3	DK, light worsted	21–24 st	5–7 / 3.75–4.5	11–15
4	Worsted, Aran	16–20 st	7–9 / 4.5–5.5	9–12
5	Bulky, chunky	12–15 st	9–11 / 5.5–8	6–9
6	Super bulky	7–11 st	11–17 / 8–12.75	5–6
7	Jumbo	6 st or less	17 and + / 12.75 and +	1–4

Closing note

That's it! You're ready to dive into the project of your choice. Of course, you still have endless techniques to learn. But you can try new things without fear because for every technique, you'll find a tutorial on my YouTube channel, CloTricots. I will be there to guide you, one stitch at a time. Until then, have fun and happy knitting!

Claudia

Crafty courses to become an expert maker...

From their studio to yours, Creative Spark instructors are teaching you how to create and become a master of your craft. So not only do you get a look inside their creative space, you also get to be a part of engaging courses that would typically be a one or multi-day workshop from the comfort of your home.

Scan for a gift from us!

Creative Spark is not your one-size-fits-all online learning experience. We welcome you to be who you are, share, create, and belong.

creativespark.ctpub.com